WOODROW & EDITH WILSON

PRESIDENTS and FIRST LADIES

iBooks
Habent Sua Fata Libelli

Ruth Ashby

Please visit our web site at:
www.ibooksforyoungreaders.com
Manhanset House
POB 342
Dering Harbor, New York 11965

Library of Congress Cataloging-in-Publication Data
Ashby, Ruth.
  Woodrow & Edith Wilson / by Ruth Ashby.
    p. cm — (Presidents and first ladies)
  Includes bibliographical references and index.

  1. Woodrow, Wilson, 1856-1924—Juvenile literature. 2. Presidents—United States—
Biography—Juvenile literature. 3. Wilson, Edith Bolling Galt, 1872-1961—Juvenile
literature. 4. Presidents' spouses—United States—Biography—Juvenile literature. 5. Married
people—United States—Biography—Juvenile literature. I. Title: Woodrow and Edith
Wilson. II. Title.

  E767.A67 2005   973.91'3'0922—dc22   [B]   2004057826

ISBN: 978-1-59687-663-7

Copyright © 2005 by Byron Preiss Visual Publications
Produced by Byron Preiss Visual Publications Inc.
Project Editor: Kelly Smith
Photo Researcher: Larry Schwartz

Photo Credits: Courtesy of the Woodrow Wilson Presidential Library: 7 (bottom), 8 (top);
Library of Congress: 4 (top and bottom), 5, 6, 7 (top), 8 (bottom), 10, 11, 12 (top and
bottom), 13, 14, 17, 18, 19, 21, 22, 23, 24, 26, 27, 29 (top and bottom), 33, 34, 36, 37, 39,
40 (top and bottom), 42; The Granger Collection, New York: 15, 16, 25, 32, 35, 41 Cover
art: The Granger Collection, New York

August 2024

CONTENTS

Words that appear in the glossary are printed in
boldface type the first time they occur in the text.

▶ INTRODUCTION ✶✶✶✶✶✶✶✶✶✶

President Woodrow Wilson in 1916.

Throughout the long night of September 25, 1919, Edith Bolling Wilson watched by the bedside of her ill husband, President Woodrow Wilson. Earlier that evening, he had summoned her to his train compartment to tell her that his headache was unbearable and something was dreadfully wrong. Now, watching his drawn face as he tried to sleep, she feared the worst. "I sat there watching the dawn break slowly," she wrote in her book, *My Memoir*, "I felt that life would never be the same . . . and from that hour on I would have to wear a mask—not only to the public but to the one I loved best in the world; for he must never know how ill he was, and I must carry on."

Edith kept her resolution. Woodrow Wilson had blazed into her life like a meteor only four years before, falling head over heels for the forty-two-year-old widow and persuading her to love again. Woodrow had also lost a spouse, his wife Ellen, and was ready for romance. As Wilson had guided the United States through World War I and led the world in a quest for peace, Edith had been at Woodrow's side. She had no doubt that her husband was the greatest man in the world, and there were many who agreed with her.

A few days later, Woodrow was felled by a paralyzing stroke, and on the advice of his doctors, Edith shielded him from the cares of his office. Her responsibility, as she saw it, was to preserve the presidency for her husband but also give him the time to recover. To this day, controversy remains about whether Edith overstepped her role as a president's wife. She, however, felt that her duty was clear. "I am not thinking of the country now," Edith said at the time. "I am thinking of my husband."

Portrait of Edith Bolling Galt Wilson, c.1915.

PATH TO GREATNESS

Thomas Woodrow Wilson was born on December 28, 1856, in Staunton, Virginia, a little more than four years before the United States was plunged into the Civil War. One of his first memories as a child was playing by the front gate of his house in 1860 and hearing a passerby say, "Mr. Lincoln is elected and there will be war." Although Tommy, as he was called, was too young to follow the war's progress, he always remembered the devastation it caused in the South—the ruined towns and shattered lives. He would always hate war, although, ironically, his life would be framed by two great conflicts.

His father, Joseph Ruggles Wilson, was a Presbyterian minister who grew up in Ohio but spent his whole professional life in the South. He moved his family from Staunton to Augusta, Georgia, in 1858 to accept a position as pastor in a large, prosperous **parish**. Woodrow Wilson would always look up to his father as the "best instructor, the most inspiring companion that a youngster ever had" and one of the great influences on his life. Joseph Wilson encouraged his son's interest in religion and politics and his love of language. His mother, Jessie Woodrow,

Thomas Woodrow Wilson in Columbia, South Carolina, in 1873, when he was about sixteen years old. He was a quiet, thoughtful-looking youth with gray-blue eyes and a long, thin face.

was an old-fashioned Southern gentlewoman, "delicate, refined," as a niece described her, and a doting mother to her four children.

A shy, thoughtful boy, young Tommy spent hours acting out scenes from adventure novels and fantasizing about ships and the sea. "I lived a dream life . . . when I was a lad," he wrote later. "All the world seemed to me a place of heroic adventure." He had difficulty learning to read, and

did not read well until he was eleven years old. Scholars today suspect that he had a learning disability and was probably **dyslexic**. Until the age of fourteen, Tommy was informally educated at home. To help him with language, his father coached him in debate. Later, when he was sixteen, Tommy taught himself **shorthand** to compensate for his disability.

A prestigious position in a **seminary** took the Reverend Wilson and his family to Columbia, South Carolina, when Tommy was fourteen. There, Tommy experienced a personal religious "awakening" that spurred a deep lifelong faith in God. Years later, when Woodrow Wilson was president, he admitted to a friend, "My life would not be worth living if it were not for the driving power of religion."

Young Scholar

In 1873, sixteen-year-old Wilson attended Davidson College in North Carolina, but remained only one year before returning home because of ill health. After a year and a half, at the recommendation of a friend, he left for the College of New Jersey, now known as Princeton. He would later describe the years at Princeton as "magical"—this was the place, he told his father, where he discovered he had a mind. He steeped himself in history, the U.S. Constitution, and the theory and practice of British and U.S. government. At Princeton, too, he first showed his natural leadership abilities, becoming the editor of the student newspaper, the *Princetonian*, and organizing a debating club. By the time he graduated, Wilson knew he had "very pronounced political ambitions."

Nassau Hall, the oldest building on the Princeton campus, as it looked when Wilson arrived in 1875.

To fulfill them, he decided to study law, for he believed that "a statesman who is unacquainted with the law is as helpless as the soldier who is ignorant of the use of arms." Wilson enrolled at the University of Virginia Law School in 1879 but soon concluded that law books were dull and dry indeed. At about this time he began to sign his letters "Woodrow Wilson," apparently deciding that "Woodrow" was a more distinguished name than "Thomas." A year after graduation, he opened up a law practice in Atlanta, Georgia, and found that he disliked the profession just as much as he thought he would. If he wanted to get into politics, he realized, it would have to be by another route. He decided instead to study history and government at the Johns Hopkins University in Baltimore, Maryland, and become a university professor.

In April 1883, Woodrow visited Rome, Georgia, on a business trip. While attending services in a local church, he spied Ellen Louise Axson, the twenty-three-year-old daughter of the Presbyterian minister. "What a bright, pretty face," Woodrow thought to himself. "I'll lay a wager this demure little lady has lots of life and fun in her." Soon they were courting, and within five months the ardent Woodrow had proposed. Lively and intelligent, Ellen was a fine painter with dreams of becoming a professional artist. She knew that if she married Woodrow, she would have to put aside her ambitions and manage a household full time, but she hoped to continue painting while raising a family.

Thomas Woodrow Wilson as a senior at Princeton, 1879.

Full of plans for the future, Wilson enrolled at Johns Hopkins in the fall of 1883 and within two years had finished his doctoral thesis, an essay entitled *Congressional Government*. It was published and earned rave reviews. "I don't believe any young man in America ever had such a brilliant triumph," Ellen wrote him proudly. On June 24, 1885, Woodrow and Ellen were married and three months later moved to Bryn Mawr, Pennsylvania, where Woodrow would teach at the brand-new women's college also called Bryn Mawr. The following April, their first child, Margaret Axson Wilson, was born, followed by two more daughters—Jessie Woodrow Wilson in August 1887, and Eleanor Randolph Wilson in 1889. Wilson was not happy at Bryn Mawr, where he found the all-female classes unstimulating. He got another job at Wesleyan College in Connecticut, which taught both male and female students, but he had been there barely two years when he realized his fondest dream: to teach at his alma mater, Princeton.

Ellen Louise Axson in 1883, the year she met Woodrow.

Princeton Star

Soon after Woodrow Wilson's arrival on the
Princeton campus in the fall of 1890, he was regarded
as one of the college's most inspiring teachers.
Students flocked to hear his witty, learned, and
wide-ranging lectures. "It was not merely a matter
of college popularity, of which Wilson enjoyed an
enormous amount," one former student remembered,
"but that we felt we had been in the presence of a
great man." While teaching law and economics at
Princeton, Wilson published many journal articles
and several books, including a biography of George
Washington in 1897 and an enormously popular
five-volume *History of the American People* in 1902.

The Wilson daughters
in 1893. From left to
right, Jessie, Eleanor,
and Margaret.

His family life was warm and satisfying, and he loved
spending time with his daughters, reading out loud to them as
his father had read to him. "I never knew anyone children liked
so much," one of his children's friends remembered. He shared a
close romantic relationship with Ellen, whom he missed
desperately whenever they were separated. "My delight in you
is so complete, my loneliness without you so irremediable, all
satisfying companionship so impossible!" he wrote her once
while away on a trip. "I literally never know what it is to have
either heart or mind satisfied, or even at rest, away from you."
For the whole Wilson family, these were happy days.

In 1902, at age forty-five, Wilson received the reward
for which he had worked so hard: He was unanimously
elected president of Princeton, which in 1896 had celebrated
its one-hundred-fiftieth anniversary by becoming a full-
fledged university with a graduate school. Woodrow Wilson

Woodrow and Ellen
Wilson in 1910,
wandering through a
Princeton garden. They
were a devoted couple
with a happy home life.

was by now so famous that his 1902 **inauguration** as president
of Princeton was attended by notables from around the country:
author Mark Twain, educator Booker T. Washington, and **financier**
J. P. Morgan. Wilson immediately put into practice a number of

reforms, raising the university's admission standards, introducing required courses, and implementing small discussion groups as well as larger lectures.

Wilson was at the height of his powers and working harder than ever when he suffered a severe shock. On the morning of May 28, 1906, he awoke to find he was blind in his left eye. Medical examinations revealed that a blood vessel had burst behind the eye and that he had had a stroke. Doctors recommended immediate rest, and Wilson and his family set off for a vacation in Britain's Lake District. Over time, some of his sight returned, but the stroke was a warning sign of health problems to come.

Visiting colleges at England's Oxford and Cambridge Universities convinced Wilson that Princeton should abolish its upper-class eating clubs—social clubs similar to fraternities—in order to attract more serious scholars. He proposed converting these clubs to residential spaces where students would live in the company of professors. His plans caused an uproar among tradition-loving alumni and under-graduates. As he was to do so often in his future political career, Wilson responded to criticism by digging in his heels and insisting he was right. The opposition grew, and his college proposal finally went down in defeat.

New Jersey Governor

Just as life at Princeton was becoming difficult, a new opportunity arose. A group of **conservative** Democratic politicians and businessmen had been watching the popular Princeton president closely and decided that he was just the man they needed as governor of New Jersey. In June 1910, they met with Wilson and persuaded him to run. All of Wilson's early political ambitions were reawakened, and on September 14, 1910, he was officially nominated by the Democratic Party. He resigned as president of the university and said good-bye to his teaching career.

Immediately Wilson defied the expectations of the men who had supported him. The New Jersey Democratic Party was run by a conservative political "machine" that supported big business against

Progressivism

Progressivism was a turn-of-the-century reform movement that evolved in response to the many problems of industrialism, including crowded cities, political corruption, business **monopolies**, and widespread poverty. It aimed to clean up government, curb the power of big business, and improve living and working conditions for lower- and middle-class citizens. The role of government, Progressives thought, was to act in the public interest.

The two most famous and effective Progressive politicians were Republican Theodore Roosevelt and Democrat Woodrow Wilson. Roosevelt, president from 1901 to 1909, called his program to ensure equal opportunity for all U.S. citizens the Square Deal. Wilson built on the progressive policies of his predecessor with the New Freedom.

Governor Wilson shakes hands with former Senator Benjamin Tillman. Almost immediately after being elected, Wilson began campaigning to secure the presidency.

the interests of workers and small farmers. Instead of advocating conservative ideas, Wilson ran on a **progressive** platform and advanced ways to make state government more responsive to the needs of working people. Wilson proposed the direct election of U.S. senators by the voters instead of by the state legislature and **primary** elections to choose presidential candidates. His ideas appealed to voters, who swept him into office with an overwhelming victory in November 1910.

Woodrow did not disappoint his supporters. At his urging, the state legislature passed a law to provide funds to workers who were injured on a job. He created a public-service committee to control railroad prices and costs for other essential public needs such as gas, water, and electricity. He established a direct presidential primary. Progressive newspaper columnist George Record wrote that in New Jersey, Wilson successfully instituted "the most remarkable record of progressive legislation ever known in the political history of this or any state."

For Wilson, though, the governorship was just a stepping stone to greater things. Across the country, people were beginning to look at him as a candidate for the presidency in the upcoming election of 1912. At the Democratic convention in June 1912, Wilson enlisted the support of William Jennings Bryan, the enormously popular midwestern politician and public speaker who had already run for president and lost three times. With Bryan's help, he took the lead from competitor Champ Clark, **Speaker of the House** from Missouri, and won the nomination. At age fifty-four, Woodrow Wilson was officially stepping out onto the national stage.

CHAPTER TWO

THE NEW FREEDOM AND A NEW WAR

The presidential race of 1912 was like no other in U.S. history. **Incumbent** president William Howard Taft, who was running on the Republican ticket, was a moderate Progressive who had been handpicked by his predecessor, Theodore Roosevelt. His administration had been so uninspired, though, that Roosevelt had turned against his former protégé and was spearheading a movement to remove Taft from office. In fact, Roosevelt had decided to run for president again himself as a nominee from the Bull Moose Party. The introduction of this third party split the Republican Party vote in two, giving Wilson and the Democratic Party a natural advantage. However, Wilson still had to differentiate himself from the dynamic and ever-popular Roosevelt.

President William Howard Taft in the spring of 1912. Taft disliked being president and ran a lackluster reelection campaign the following fall.

Wilson and Roosevelt were both Progressives. They both favored curbing big business, improving the rights of workers, and eventually giving women the right to vote. Roosevelt, however, wanted to limit the power of big corporations by appointing a new government commission to oversee business. Wilson thought it would be less expensive simply to break up some of the corporations, thereby offering smaller businesses the chance to compete. He would pass laws, he promised, that would bring back free enterprise and "prevent the strong from crushing the weak." He called his domestic program the New Freedom. The man who had been the best lecturer at Princeton now wowed crowds at county fairs and town halls with his eloquence.

On Election Day, November 5, 1912, Wilson and his family were in Princeton when he received the news via telegraph that he had won

Theodore Roosevelt, 1910. Although Roosevelt and Wilson were both Progressives, they were rivals in the presidential election of 1912. After former president Roosevelt was hospitalized following an attempted assassination in October, Wilson cut short his campaign engagements out of respect.

the race. He had gained 6.3 million votes, compared to 4.1 million for Roosevelt and 3.5 million for Taft. Although Wilson did not win a majority of popular votes, he had 435 **electoral college** votes, with 11 for Roosevelt and 8 for Taft. It was an impressive victory.

The Triumph of Progressivism

On Inauguration Day, Wilson drove to the Capitol with outgoing president Taft, who was in a very cheerful mood. "I'm glad to be going," Taft told Wilson. "This is the loneliest place in the world."

For the next few years, Wilson pushed hard to see some of his progressive ideas become law. First, he pushed a bill through Congress that lowered the tariff, or tax, on goods coming into the country. This law would increase competition, he claimed, and lower the cost of goods for U.S. consumers. To make up for the loss of revenue, he took advantage of the passing of the Sixteenth Amendment in 1913, which allowed Congress to pass an income tax. Wilson instituted the first permanent income tax on incomes of more than $3,000 (in today's dollars about $54,567).

Next, he regulated the nation's banking system by establishing the Federal Reserve Board. Control of the banking system, Wilson told Congress on June 23, 1913, must be "public, not private, must be vested in the government itself, so that the banks must be the instruments, not the masters, of business." Financial experts on the board would set **interest rates** and issue money. *The New York Times* hailed the Federal Reserve Act as a "**Magna Carta** of political and industrial liberty under a government by law," the most important finance bill since the Civil War.

President-elect Woodrow Wilson and outgoing President William Howard Taft share a laugh before Wilson's inauguration on March 4, 1913. Taft proceeded to have a distinguished career as a Supreme Court judge.

When Wilson turned his attention to reforming big business, he discovered that it was not as easy to break up large corporations as he had hoped. Instead, he pushed Congress to pass laws that would control big business and give small business a chance to compete. In September 1914, Congress established the Federal Trade Commission, which had the power to order companies to stop practicing unfair business competition. A month later, it passed the Clayton Antitrust Act, which outlawed certain business practices such as local price-cutting designed to scare away outside competition and gave people the right to join unions without being prosecuted.

According to historians, the first two years of Wilson's presidency saw the passage of more important legislation than at any time since George Washington's term in office. In addition to regulating business, Wilson also passed laws that limited working hours for children and established compensation for workers injured on a job. Yet by the fall of 1914, the progress of the New Freedom program was interrupted by a series of personal and international disasters that would change Wilson's presidency irrevocably.

Shadows Fall

At first, the Wilson family was very happy in the White House. Ellen, kind and efficient, was an immediate favorite with the staff. Even in the White House, she was able to make time for her painting, and her portraits and landscapes were shown in an exhibition of notable women artists. Always interested in social work, she made **slum** clearance her special project when she witnessed the rundown housing in Washington's African-American community. Ellen personally took congressmen on a tour of the area and gave her backing to a bill that would destroy the old buildings and finance new housing.

The Wilson family in 1913, during the summer of Wilson's first term. From left to right: Margaret, Ellen, Nell, Jessie, and Woodrow.

13

She and Woodrow had lost none of their devotion to each other over the years, and when they were separated for part of the summer of 1913, they reaffirmed their love by letter. "It seems to me that I have never loved you as I do now!" Woodrow wrote his wife from the isolation of the White House. "I am certainly the most fortunate man alive." From her rented home in Cornish, New Hampshire, Ellen replied, "Your wonderful, your adorable Sunday letter has just come and has made me fairly drunk with happiness. I would give anything to be able to express my love as perfectly as you do. . . . God bless you, my darling, my darling."

That November there was a huge wedding in the White House, with more than one thousand guests, when daughter Jessie married young lawyer Francis B. Sayre. A few months later, the engagement of Eleanor "Nell" Wilson to Secretary of the Treasury William

The wedding portrait of Eleanor "Nell" Wilson, May 1914. The next spring, Nell gave Woodrow his first grandchild, a little girl named Ellen after Nell's mother.

Gibbs McAdoo was announced. The ceremony was delayed when Ellen took a bad fall in March 1914. Though it seemed to take her a long time to recover, she was present, pale but resolute, for the wedding on May 7. Afterward, however, she went into a steady decline, and by mid-June Ellen was so weak she could no longer get out of bed. Woodrow kept constant vigil, insisting that she was only depressed and would recover.

Woodrow kept Ellen up to date on the situation in Mexico, about which she was vitally interested. Mexico had been in a civil war since May 1911; and Wilson despised the new Mexican president, a brutal man named Victoriano Huerta. When Huerta arrested the crew of a U.S. whaleboat in April 1914, Wilson retaliated by seizing the Mexican port of Veracruz. In the fight, nineteen U.S. soldiers were killed. Argentina, Brazil, and Chile offered to mediate between the two nations, and Wilson demanded the removal of Huerta from

Mexico

Victoriano Huerta's departure from Mexico in July 1914 did not end Mexico's Revolution or the U.S. involvement with its troubled neighbor. General Pancho Villa, who had helped Venustiano Carranza overthrow Huerta, tried in turn to overthrow Carranza, who was supported by the United States. In January 1916, Villa's bandits attacked a train in northern Mexico and shot seventeen U.S. citizens. Two months later, Villa invaded the town of Columbus, New Mexico, killing nineteen Americans.

Wilson promised immediate retaliation. General John J. Pershing and a force of four thousand U.S. troops pursued Villa across the Mexican border.

When several months passed without Villa's capture, Carranza demanded that the U.S. troops withdraw. Skirmishes between Mexican and U.S. troops threatened all-out war, but neither Wilson nor Carranza were willing to take such a drastic step.

Finally, the two nations reached an agreement, and in February 1917, Pershing withdrew without ever locating Pancho Villa.

Revolutionary Mexican leader Francisco "Pancho Villa" (left) at the head of his troops in 1914. Villa retired to a ranch near Hidalgo del Parral, Mexico, where he was assassinated in 1923.

power. In July, rebel troops under the command of Venustiano Carranza and Pancho Villa defeated Huerta. Huerta fled Mexico, and the crisis was past. Perhaps, Wilson hoped, Mexico was on its way to **democracy**.

The Lights Go Out

In late June, a far worse international situation developed. On June 28, 1914, Austrian Archduke Franz Ferdinand and his wife Sophie were assassinated by a Serbian nationalist in Sarajevo, Bosnia. With this one fatal act, Europe was plunged into a conflict that escalated into a world war—hailed at the time as the Great War and now called World War I. One by one, the major European powers called on their allies and assembled their armies. Austria-Hungary, determined to punish Serbia for the assassination, officially declared war on July 28, 1914, and Russia rushed in to defend its ally, Serbia.

On August 1, 1914, Austria's ally, Germany, in turn declared war on Russia and on Russia's ally, France, two days later. "The sword has been forced into our hands," Germany's Kaiser Wilhelm II insisted.

On August 2, 1914, German troops were massed on the Belgian border, ready to march through the country on their way to France. Great Britain, which had vowed to defend Belgium against aggression, declared war on Germany on August 4. In his office at dusk, British foreign secretary Edmund Gray made a famous prophecy: "The lamps are going out all over Europe; we shall not see them lit again in our lifetime."

When he found out that Austria had declared war, Wilson murmured to his daughter Nell, "I can think of nothing—nothing, when my dear one is suffering." Nonetheless, as he sat by Ellen's bedside, he drafted an offer to act as negotiator between the hostile parties.

Woodrow was lost in grief, for now it was obvious that his beloved wife was going to die. Ellen was diagnosed with Bright's disease, a kidney disorder, and also with **tuberculosis** of the kidneys. On August 4, White House physician Dr. Cary Grayson advised Woodrow to summon the family to say goodbye. Ellen's last wish was that Congress pass her slum clearance bill. At Wilson's request, Congress pushed the bill through. On August 6, 1914, while Woodrow held her hand and her daughters prayed, Ellen Axson Wilson died.

"Oh, my God, what am I going to do?" he murmured.

Archduke Franz Ferdinand and Archduchess Sophie of Austria prepare to join a royal procession in Sarajevo, Bosnia, on June 28, 1914. Moments later, as their automobile rolled through the streets, a Serbian assassin named Gavrilo Princip jumped on the running board and shot them both to death.

Woodrow struggled not to break down during the next few days as he sat vigil by Ellen, attended the funeral service in the East Room of the White House, and accompanied the coffin to Ellen's hometown of Rome, Georgia, where she would be buried. Not until the coffin was lowered into the ground did he begin to sob. For months afterward, he remained sunk in grief, "dead in heart and body, weighed down with a leaden indifference and despair," as he wrote a friend. Wilson even confessed to his good friend Colonel Edward House that he didn't want to live anymore. Only work and the necessity of doing his duty kept him going.

Meanwhile, the crisis in Europe had to be dealt with. The mood in the United States was strongly **isolationist**, and people did not want the United States to become involved with the catastrophe developing across the Atlantic. Wilson called on Americans to be "impartial in thought as well as action." Remaining truly neutral was difficult to maintain. Most Americans favored the Allied forces—Britain, France, Belgium, and Russia. Some Americans of German or Austrian descent, especially in the Midwest, sympathized with the Central powers—Germany, Austria-Hungary, and the Ottoman, or Turkish, Empire. Wilson himself disliked the aggressive German government and found himself automatically favoring the Allies. In 1915, he permitted powerful financiers such as J. P. Morgan to give $2 billion in loans to the Allies.

As Europe turned into one vast battlefield, Wilson recovered from the worst of his grief and found himself looking forward to spring. One day in February 1915, he was out driving with Dr. Grayson when Grayson waved to a friend. "Who is that beautiful lady?" Wilson asked. A few weeks later, he would meet the beautiful lady herself in the White House, and he would be reborn. Her name was Edith Bolling Galt.

Ellen Axson Wilson in 1912. She was a gracious and committed first lady for more than a year and a half.

A SOUTHERN GIRL

Edith Bolling was born in the small town of Wytheville, Virginia, on October 15, 1872, the seventh of eleven children of Judge William Holcombe Bolling and Sallie White Bolling. She came from an old Virginia family that traced its roots back to the seventeenth century; in fact, on her father's side, Edith was descended from Pocahontas, the Native American princess. Pocahontas and English planter John Rolfe had one son, Thomas. His daughter Jane married Colonel Robert Bolling. Seven generations later, Edith was born.

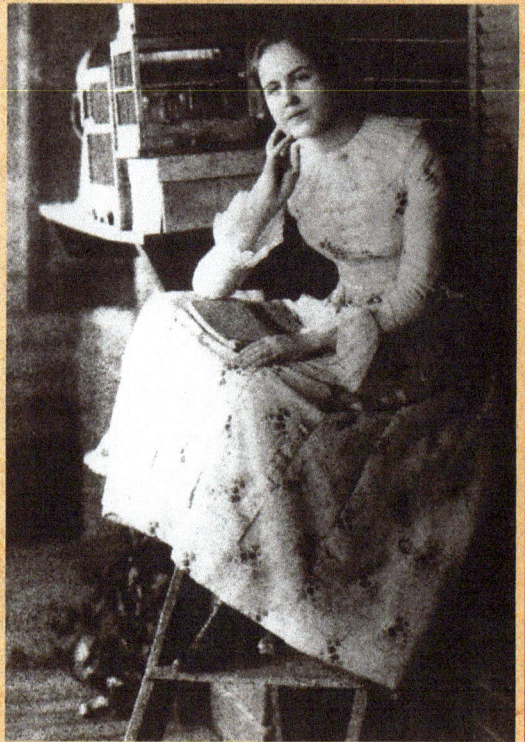

Edith Bolling in a pensive moment at age fifteen, seated on the porch of her family's home in Wytheville, Virginia.

Before the Civil War, the Bollings had been reasonably well-to-do plantation owners. After the war, with their slaves freed and no one to work on the farm, they moved to an old brick house in Wytheville where two grandmothers, two aunts, and eleven children lived under one roof. "Though the house was shabby and inadequate," Edith remembered later, "material deficiencies were repaired by understanding, sympathy, and love, making it to us healthy, happy youngsters in every sense a home."

Grandmother Bolling took Edith under her wing. A tiny woman of fierce principles and inflexible judgment, Grandmother Bolling had injured her back years before and now kept court in a big room in the center of the house. "I can truly say she taught me nearly everything I know," Edith recalled. Under her grandmother's strict guidance and instruction, Edith learned to read and write, "to knit, to sew, to embroider, hemstich and crochet, and to cut and fit dresses." In turn, Edith waited on her grandmother night and day, slept in her big four-poster bed, and cared for her twenty-six canaries.

Edith had no formal education, however, until she was fifteen, when she went to boarding school at Martha Washington College in Abingdon, Virginia. Though Edith had planned to study music, the rooms at the college were so cold that her fingers were too stiff to play the piano. Her thin, boney appearance in her gray dress caused her classmates to call her the gray spider. When her parents heard about the harsh conditions at the school, they brought her home. During the following winter of 1888, she went to another boarding school, Mrs. Powell's School in Richmond, that she liked much better. She could stay no longer than a year, however, because her father had three younger sons to educate and could not afford to keep his daughter in school. As a result, Edith had only two years of formal schooling altogether.

A Wife and a Widow

Instead of returning to school in the fall of 1889, Edith traveled to Washington, D.C., to visit her married sister Gertrude. One evening, after going to hear renowned singer Adelina Patti in concert, Edith arrived home to find Norman Galt, her brother-in-law's cousin, sitting in the dining room eating oysters from a chafing dish. Norman's family owned the most successful jewelry and fine silver business in Washington.

Norman fell in love with Edith and for the next few years courted her with chocolates, flowers, and friendship. He was nine years older than Edith, who was only eighteen when they met and not ready to get married. By the time she was twenty-four, she

Edith Bolling Galt in 1899. She looks every inch the wife of a prosperous Washington, D.C., merchant.

realized it was time to make a decision, even though she was not really in love. Edith Bolling and Norman Galt married in 1896.

Within two years, a series of deaths left Norman in charge of the family business. Then in 1903, Edith and Norman experienced a piercing loss when their son of three days died, and Edith was told she would have no more children. Within five years, Norman died of a liver ailment, making Edith the sole owner of Galt and Brother, Inc.

An Independent Woman

Edith depended on the store to support herself, her widowed mother, a sister, and three brothers. With the help of the store manager, Edith took on the job of running the business herself. Now independent and well-to-do, she traveled to Europe every summer with friends and became the first woman in Washington, D.C., to drive around in an electric car.

One of her traveling companions was Alice Gertrude Gordon, or Altrude, a young woman who was being ardently pursued by President Wilson's personal physician, Dr. Cary Grayson. The White House had become a quiet, mournful place, Grayson told them, where Wilson and his cousin, Helen Bones, who acted as his companion and occasional hostess, lived alone. One day in early 1915, Grayson asked Edith if she would mind accompanying Helen on occasional walks. During their long jaunts in Rock Creek Park, Helen told Edith all about the lonely man in the White House, and Edith found her sympathy stirred. However, she recalled, "I felt he was too remote for me ever to have an opportunity to know and assay for myself."

After one of these walks in March 1915, Helen asked her new friend to come back to the White House for some tea. Edith hesitated. What if she ran into the president by mistake? She wasn't dressed for company, and her boots were all muddy. Helen assured her that Wilson was out playing golf.

That afternoon, as Edith was coming out of the White House elevator, she "turned a corner and met [her] fate."

A NEW LIFE

When Edith Bolling Galt and Helen Bones stepped off the elevator, they came face to face with Woodrow Wilson and Cary Grayson, who had just returned from their golf game. Edith was pleased to see that their boots were just as muddy as hers. Helen invited the gentlemen to join them for tea, and before Edith knew it, she was sitting and chatting with the president of the United States.

Edith Bolling Galt in February 1915, just before she met Woodrow Wilson.

Sixteen years older than she, Wilson was tall, spare, and energetic. His gray-blue eyes lit up with intelligence when he spoke. At forty-two, Edith was a delightfully attractive woman, with dark hair, gray eyes, and, the president soon discovered, a great deal of personal charm. He was immediately taken with her.

Edith was invited back to join Helen and Woodrow for dinner a few nights later, then for numerous car rides and chats. On April 28, 1915, Woodrow sent her a book she had asked for. "I hope it will give you a little pleasure," he wrote. "I covet nothing more than to give you pleasure—you have given me so much!" A week later, on May 4, he sat with Edith alone on the south portico of the White House, drew his chair close to hers, and told her that he loved her and wanted to marry her. For Edith, the revelation came as a shock.

"Oh, you can't love me," she blurted out, "for you don't really know me; and it is less than a year since your wife died."

Woodrow explained gently that he would not be a gentleman if he did not let her know his intentions from the start of their relationship. As president, he could not visit her unaccompanied;

she would always have to come to him. For this reason, he had already told his daughters and Helen of his feelings, so that they could arrange for her to see him.

Edith left that night filled with emotion. She stayed up for hours writing him a letter, letting Woodrow know that she was not turning him down but seeking to know him better. "Here on this white page I pledge you all that is best in me," she promised him, "to help, to sustain, to comfort—and that into the space that separates us I send my spirit to seek yours."

Encouraged by her response, Woodrow wrote back a wistful letter: "Here stands your friend, a longing man, in the midst of a world's affairs—a world that knows nothing of the heart he has shown you . . . but which he cannot face with his full strength or with the fullest of keen endeavors unless you come into that heart and take possession, not because it is exposed but because, simply and only because, you love him. *Can* you love him?"

The Threat of War

On May 7, 1915, the day after Edith received Woodrow's letter, a German **U-boat,** or submarine, torpedoed a British passenger ship, the *Lusitania,* near the coast of Ireland. The German government had previously declared all the waters around Great Britain a war

The ocean liner *Lusitania* was hit off the coast of Ireland by a torpedo from a German U-boat. A subsequent interior explosion caused the great ship to sink in only twenty minutes. Altogether, 1,198 men, women, and children died.

zone and warned the world that any ship entering the area could be attacked. Within twenty minutes the great ship sank, killing 1,198 out of the 1,959 people on board, 128 of them U.S. citizens.

Outraged people across the United States called the sinking of the *Lusitania* deliberate murder. Although angry, Wilson proceeded cautiously, aware that although the people were upset, they still did not want to go to war. After calm consideration, he sent Germany a protest demanding a stop to the attacks on neutral vessels and passenger ships. When the German government defended its actions, he sent another, more strongly worded letter.

Wilson kept Edith informed about every step of the negotiations, and she gave him her advice. After a rapidly proceeding courtship, they became secretly engaged on September 3, 1915. Nearly every

The Western Front

World War I was fought all around the world—in Europe, Asia, Africa, and the South Pacific. Most of the important battles took place on the Western Front, however. In the first Battle of the Marne, September 6–9, 1914, the French Army halted the German advance, and both sides dug in along a line of trenches that eventually stretched about 400 miles (644 kilometers) from Switzerland north through France and Belgium to the English Channel.

Month after month, troops hunkered down in the muddy, disease-ridden trenches, each about 6 to 8 feet (2 meters) deep. Between the trenches was a barren area of mines and barbed wire known as no-man's land. During an attack, soldiers had to cross no-man's land in the face of blistering enemy fire.

Battles were weeks, even months, long and extremely costly in human lives. In the Battle of the Somme (July to November 1916), for instance,

British casualties totaled 400,000, French casualties 200,000, and Germans casualties 450,000—and the Allies gained merely 5 miles (8 km). It was no wonder that U.S. citizens, appalled by the carnage, did not want to get involved.

Entrenched Swiss soldiers prepare to attack the enemy, c.1915. Allied and German soldiers alike spent months at a time living in the trenches, where they were exposed to all sorts of weather and tormented by rats, bugs, and diseases.

day he sent her an orchid. "You are the only woman I know who can wear an orchid," he told her. "On everybody else the orchid wears the woman."

Wilson's careful foreign diplomacy continued until August 19, 1915, when the passenger ship *Arabic* was sunk by German U-boats, again with U.S. casualties. This time Wilson threatened to cut off diplomatic relations with Germany if it did not renounce its actions. Two weeks later, Germany finally agreed to halt aggression against unarmed ships. For the moment at least, the United States would not go to war.

Wedding Vows

All that summer, Woodrow and Edith wrote each other daily, expressing their love and discussing politics. When Edith went on vacation with some friends, Woodrow sent her important government papers to read, marked with his comments. He was

This romantic collage of Edith Bolling Galt and Woodrow Wilson appeared in a Washington newspaper after their engagement was announced. Edith is adorned with her trademark orchid.

educating her to be the wife of a president, someone to whom he could open his heart about not only private but also public matters. Edith was pleased to be trusted. "Much as I enjoy your delicious love letters," she wrote him, "I believe I enjoy even more the ones in which you tell me what you are working on—the things that fill your thoughts and demand your best effort. For then I feel I am sharing your work and being taken into partnership, as it were."

Wilson's advisors felt strongly that he should wait to remarry, that the American public would never forgive him for falling in love so soon after Ellen's death. But the couple was eager to tell their news, and in early October 1915, their engagement was announced. Most citizens were glad their president had found happiness. The people of California sent Edith a large nugget of gold to make into a wedding ring, and crowds at the Baker Bowl National League Park in Philadelphia gave them a noisy welcome when they arrived to see a World Series game. One night after Woodrow had been to Edith's home for dinner, he startled a Secret Service agent by "dancing off the curbs and up them as we crossed streets. . . . He whistled softly through his teeth, tapping out the rhythm with restless feet: 'Oh, you beautiful doll! You great big beautiful doll!'"

On December 18, 1915, Woodrow and Edith were married in a small family ceremony at Edith's home. The groom looked dapper in a cutaway coat and striped trousers; the bride wore black velvet and white orchids. Afterward, they sneaked off for a secret honeymoon in Hot Springs, Virginia.

A Second Term

In the presidential election of 1916, Wilson was running against the backdrop of war. America's shipping was under attack, and its neutrality was being strongly tested. In March 1916, the Germans broke their

A Woodrow Wilson campaign button from his 1916 reelection campaign.

Charles Evans Hughes, Republican candidate for president in the election of 1916. He was a former New York governor and associate justice of the Supreme Court who ran on a progressive platform.

pledge by sinking a French ferry boat called the *Sussex*, killing dozens of civilians and wounding four Americans. Wilson again threatened to cut off diplomatic relations. Facing the fact that war remained a possibility, he passed a National Defense Act in spring 1916 that provided for a larger and more prepared Army and Navy.

Wilson's opponent in the presidential race would be Republican Charles Evan Hughes, who served as an associate justice of the Supreme Court. Wilson stressed that his record spoke for itself: reform legislation at home and neutrality abroad. "He kept us out of war!" was his campaign's rallying cry. Wilson, however, realized how tenuous the peace actually was. "I can't keep the country out of war," he confided to secretary of the U.S. Navy, Josephus Daniels. "They talk of me as though I were a god. Any little German lieutenant can put us into the war at any time by some calculated outrage."

Edith proved to be a skillful campaigner, able to use her natural people-skills to charm voters and politicians alike. On election day, the Wilsons gathered at their rented home on the New Jersey shore to await the returns. The race was very tight, and at first it looked as if Hughes was going to beat Wilson by a slim margin. The morning after the election, *The New York Times* headlines proclaimed, "Charles E. Hughes Has Apparently Been Elected President." Not until two days later was it confirmed that California had come through for the president and that Wilson had beaten Hughes by 591,385 votes. He squeaked by with 277 electoral votes, as opposed to Hughes's 254. Woodrow Wilson was staying in the White House.

OVER THERE

His reelection assured, Wilson launched a major effort to end the war and bring peace. On January 22, 1917, Wilson addressed the Senate and argued that the European troops should choose a "peace without victory," a general **disarmament** and freedom of the seas. "Victory would mean peace forced upon the loser," he explained, "and would leave a sting, a resentment, a bitter memory upon which terms of peace would rest, not permanently, but only as upon quicksand." It would be far better to have a peace among equals.

Both the Allied forces and the Central powers rejected the idea of anything but total victory. Then, two events dashed Wilson's last hope of remaining neutral. On February 1, Germany announced that it would wage unrestricted submarine warfare, including on passenger vessels. Even though German leaders realized their actions would probably bring the United States into the war, they were betting that they could win before the United States sent its troops into action.

A cartoon showing Kaiser Wilhelm II of Germany tearing up the German agreement not to use submarines to attack civilian ships. Drawing by J. H. Cassel for the *Evening World Daily Magazine*, February 2, 1917.

Subsequently, on February 25, British intelligence passed along a coded telegram intercepted from German Foreign Secretary Arthur Zimmerman to the German ambassador in Mexico. It proposed that Mexico become Germany's ally in case the United States declared war on Germany. In return, Germany promised Mexico its "lost territory in New Mexico, Texas, and Arizona"—territory the United States had won in the Mexican War of 1846–48. In the face of public outrage over this message, Wilson cut diplomatic relations with Germany.

Events catapulted forward. Immediately, as Wilson had feared, Germany began to sink U.S. ships. In her diary, Edith wrote, "The shadow of war is stretching its dark length over our country." Then, revolutionaries in Russia rebelled against the **czar** and overthrew him. The Allies hoped the new Russian government would be a democracy. They could then claim that the war was a fight between democracies and the **militaristic autocracies** of Germany and Austria-Hungary.

If the United States had to go to war, Wilson thought, it would be for a noble cause—the cause of democracy. He was up all night on April 1, 1917, readying his war message, while Edith kept him company and brought him milk and cookies. The next day, a grim-faced Wilson addressed a special session of Congress and asked them to declare war on the Central powers "to make the world safe for democracy." The route back to the White House was lined with hundreds of thousands of people holding candles and waving American flags. On April 6, both houses of Congress voted for war 455 to 56, and Wilson signed the declaration with a golden pen.

Unfortunately, in November 1917, **communists** under Vladimir Lenin overthrew the Provisional Russian government. Lenin promptly made a separate treaty with Germany, and Russia withdrew from the war.

Combat Ready

America's entry into the war came none too soon for the Allies. Their troops were weary and disheartened, and German U-boats were sinking one out of every four ships that left an Allied port. Britain was down to a few weeks' supply of food. The U.S. Army, with only 126,000 men in uniform, was not ready to fight, however. In May 1917, Congress passed a Selective Service Act that required all men between the ages of 21 and 30 to register for military service. Within a month, 2.2 million men had been drafted, and 4 million would eventually serve. General John J. "Black Jack" Pershing was given command of the American Expeditionary Force

(AEF), which sent the first U.S. soldiers to France in June 1917.

Under Wilson's leadership, the United States readied itself for war. To raise money for the war effort, Congress raised taxes and encouraged citizens to lend money to the government by buying "Liberty Bonds." The War Industries Board regulated the economy by setting prices and monitoring production, and the War Labor Board settled labor disputes and kept workers from striking. The Food Administration, headed by engineer and future president Herbert Hoover, was in charge of raising food production and encouraging consumers to limit their food intake in order to send more to the troops.

A 1917 poster urging patriotic Americans to help finance the war by buying Liberty Bonds. Two-thirds of the cost of the war—$23 billion—was paid for by people who bought government-backed bonds, savings certificates, and stamps

Like other Americans, the Wilsons observed "wheatless Mondays" and "meatless Tuesdays." Edith organized a Red Cross sewing group at the White House that made pajamas and wool hats for the soldiers overseas. To free up the White House gardener for war work, Edith bought a herd of sheep to graze on the lawn and keep the grass short. The sheep multiplied, their coats were shorn, and their wool was auctioned off by the Red Cross for the incredible amount of almost $100,000 (in today's dollars about $1.3 million).

As always, Edith devoted herself to helping Woodrow any way she could. He encouraged her to learn the private code used by the State Department in foreign communications, and she coded and decoded Woodrow's messages for him. Her most important job, she soon realized,

Edith Wilson's sheep and lambs graze on the White House lawn, c.1918. She remembered later that "children would stand for hours outside the fence to watch them."

was helping her overworked husband to relax. She had always gone golfing with him. Now, to give him more exercise, she also took up horseback riding, and even tried to ride a bicycle, which she had never learned to do when she was a girl. She didn't learn now, either, but her doomed attempts kept them both laughing and lighthearted.

Wilson knew how easily civil liberties such as freedom of the press could erode during time of war. "Once lead this people into war," he told the editor of the New York *World*, "and they'll forget there ever was such a thing as tolerance." Wilson clearly recognized the dangers of extreme patriotism, but he failed to curb the excesses of the war movement crusade. The Committee on Public Information started a propaganda campaign against all things German: the German language, German music, German books. German sauerkraut was even renamed "liberty cabbage." Wilson called such ideas "ridiculous and childish," but could not stop the spread of intolerance. Yet even he supported the Sedition Act of 1918, which fined and sent people to jail for criticizing the government.

The Fourteen Points

On January 8, 1918, Wilson presented his peace proposal to a joint session of Congress. He wanted not only to establish a "just and lasting peace" for this war, he stated, but also to prevent future wars. Already Wilson knew that Britain and France were plotting to exact revenge on Germany and Austria-Hungary, perhaps even to split their territory between them. Although the fighting was far from over, he realized that publicizing his vision would give the war-weary citizens of Europe some hope for the future. His blueprint for peace, known as the "Fourteen Points," was studied by people around the world.

In the first point, he proposed that any peace treaty be open and public. The next four points had to do with freedom of the seas, freedom of trade, arms limitations, and the settlement of **colonial** disputes. Then, in the next eight points, Wilson turned to the question of national boundaries. The peoples of the world, he declared, should have the right of self-determination—the right

Wilson's Fourteen Points

I. "Open covenants of peace, openly arrived at . . .

II. Absolute freedom of navigation upon the seas . . .

III. The removal . . . of all economic barriers and the establishment of an equality of trade conditions among all the nations consenting to the peace . . .

IV. Adequate guarantees given and taken that national armaments will be reduced . . .

V. A free, open-minded, and absolutely impartial adjustment of all colonial claims . . .

VI. The evacuation of all Russian territory and such a settlement of all questions affecting Russia as will secure the best and freest cooperation of the other nations of the world in obtaining for her an . . . opportunity for the independent determination of her own political development and national policy . . .

VII. Belgium . . . must be evacuated and restored, without any attempt to limit the sovereignty which she enjoys in common with all other free nations. . . .

VIII. All French territory should be freed and the invaded portions restored . . .

IX. A readjustment of the frontiers of Italy should be effected along clearly recognizable lines of nationality.

X. The peoples of Austria-Hungary . . . should be accorded the freest opportunity to autonomous development.

XI. Rumania, Serbia, and Montenegro should be evacuated; occupied territories restored . . . and the relations of the several Balkan states to one another determined by friendly counsel along historically established lines of allegiance and nationality . . .

XII. The Turkish portion of the present Ottoman Empire should be assured a secure sovereignty, but the other nationalities which are now under Turkish rule should be assured of . . . an absolutely unmolested opportunity of autonomous development . . .

XIII. An independent Polish state should be erected which should include the territories inhabited by indisputably Polish populations . . .

XIV. A general association of nations must be formed under specific covenants for the purpose of affording mutual guarantees of political independence and territorial integrity to great and small states alike."

to choose their own nations and type of government. Lastly, in the fourteenth point, Wilson proposed an international association of countries called the League of Nations to protect "mutual guarantees of political independence and territorial integrity to great and small states alike." To Wilson, the league was a crucial element of the peace effort, for he believed its establishment would prevent a world war from ever happening again.

The War Nears its End

By March 1918, German troops were on the offensive and pushing through Allied lines toward Paris. At the time, fewer than 300,000 U.S. troops were on the Western Front, but by June that number reached one million. For the first time, at the battle of Belleau Wood in France, the Americans made a difference in the war, forcing the Germans out of their **entrenchments**. When the German Army made an all-out attempt to take Paris in mid-July, they were halted by the U.S. forces in three days of fierce fighting.

As U.S. soldiers kept pouring into the front lines, the tide of war began to turn. On September 26, 1918, the Allies launched an offensive in the Argonne Forest, a hilly, heavily wooded area between the Meuse River in France and Belgium. It took forty-seven days, but the U.S. and French forces finally smashed through the German lines and captured forty-eight thousand prisoners and a railroad junction. The Meuse-Argonne offensive and numerous other successful Allied campaigns in eastern Europe and the Middle East finally broke the German government's resolve. Starving at home and losing on the battlefield, the Germans realized their hope of victory was gone.

French gunners man a large cannon in the Argonne Forest during World War I.

In early October, Germany proposed an armistice, or end to the fighting. Wilson, however, would not set a date until the German emperor stepped down and the Allies and Germany agreed to accept the Fourteen Points. On November 9, 1918, Kaiser Wilhelm II resigned, and the Allies and Germans reluctantly accepted Wilson's terms. The armistice was signed on November 11, 1918, at 11:00 A.M.—the eleventh hour of the eleventh day of the eleventh month. The Great War—what Wilson hoped would be "the war to end all wars"—was over.

More than 10 million soldiers had died on the battlefield, about 50,000 of them from the United States, and about 21 million were wounded. No one knows how many civilians died. Most of northern France and parts of Belgium were bombed-out wastelands, and hundreds of thousands of people had lost their homes, farms, and businesses. The Allies blamed all the destruction on Germany, and no matter what Wilson said, they wanted their former enemy to pay.

CHAPTER SIX

THE LAST CRUSADE

President Wilson was determined to go to Paris to negotiate the peace treaty himself. On December 4, 1918, he and Edith sailed with the rest of the U.S. peace delegation on the liner *George Washington* from Hoboken, New Jersey. Edith's private secretary, Edith Benham, noticed how devoted the Wilsons were to each other. "The more I am with the Wilsons," she remarked, "the more I am struck with their unrivaled home life. I have never dreamed such sweetness and love could be. . . . It is very beautiful to see his face light up and brighten at the very sight of her and to see her turn to him for everything."

In Paris in December 1918, Woodrow and Edith Wilson were welcomed with flags, flowers, and ecstatic, cheering crowds. Here they greet well-wishers from the backseat of an open carriage.

In 1918, "*Wilson le Juste*" (Wilson the Just), as the French called him, was the most honored man in the world, and all of Europe wanted to pay him homage. Years later, Edith remembered that when she and the president arrived, Paris "was wild with celebration. Every inch was covered with cheering, shouting humanity. The sidewalks, the buildings, even the stately horse-chestnut trees were peopled with men and boys perched like sparrows in their very tops. Roofs were filled, windows overflowed until one grew giddy trying to greet the bursts of welcome that came like the surging of untamed waters. Flowers rained upon us until we were nearly buried." Next they traveled to London where they were met at the railroad station by King George V and Queen Mary, who led them in a triumphant procession to Buckingham Palace. When they visited Rome, the streets were covered with golden sands from the Mediterranean Sea, an ancient tribute to conquering heroes.

Women's Suffrage

The women's suffrage movement began in Seneca Falls, New York, in 1848. After a half of a century of holding rallies and lobbying Congress, by 1912 women still did not have the right to vote in federal elections. Although Wilson said he was for women's suffrage, his support was lukewarm. For a year and a half during World War I, suffragettes picketed the White House daily. "Mr. President, How Long Must Women Wait for Liberty?" one of their banners read.

The suffrage campaign and women's contributions to the war effort finally convinced Wilson that they deserved the vote. On September 30, 1918, he urged the Senate to pass the women's suffrage amendment: "We shall need them in our vision of affairs as we have never needed them before," he said, "the sympathy and insight and clear moral instinct of the women of the world." The Nineteenth Amendment was passed by Congress the following summer and **ratified** by the states on August 18, 1920.

Suffragettes picket in front of the White House, February 1917. Between June and November 1917, 218 women were arrested on charges of "obstructing sidewalk traffic" outside the gates. After leader Alice Paul was jailed, she went on a hunger strike and was force-fed by guards. In the face of all the negative publicity, Wilson finally backed down and supported the suffrage amendment.

A Difficult Peace

The Peace Conference opened at the Versailles Palace outside Paris on January 18, 1919. Wilson had come to Europe believing that the other Big Four nations—Great Britain, France, and Italy—had accepted the Fourteen Points. In fact, they wanted to renegotiate everything. Georges Clemenceau, the French prime minister, was determined to do anything he could to keep Germans from ever invading French soil again. Together with British prime minister David Lloyd George and Italian prime minister Vittorio Orlando, he wanted Germany to pay for the damages inflicted by the war and to accept responsibility for starting it.

The conference exhausted Wilson, despite Edith and Dr. Grayson's attempts to make sure he got enough exercise and sleep. At the end of

March, he became violently ill with a high fever, which experts now think may have been a form of **encephalitis**. Afterward, observers noted, he became irritable more often and was obsessed with controlling small details. He drove himself relentlessly to bring all the participants to agreement.

Georges Clemenceau (front, left, holding his hat and cane), Woodrow Wilson (center) and Lloyd George (far right holding his hat above his head) leave the palace of Versailles after finally signing a peace treaty, June 28, 1919.

In the ensuing months, Wilson was forced to compromise, conceding some points in return for keeping the League of Nations. Most important, he had to give up the idea of "peace without victory." Harsh terms were imposed on Germany, which was not even allowed to attend the conference. The final treaty forced Germany to sign a "war guilt" clause accepting complete responsibility for the war and to agree to pay $15 billion (in today's dollars about $160 billion) in reparations.

Wilson did see his idea of self-determination bear partial fruit, however, at least in Europe. The nations of Yugoslavia, Czechoslovakia, Poland, Lithuania, Latvia, Estonia, and Finland were carved out of the old empires of Germany, Austria-Hungary, and Russia. And, most crucial to Wilson, the League of Nations was established. "A living thing is born," Wilson stated. "It is definitely a guarantee of peace."

On June 28, 1919, the Treaty of Versailles was signed in the Hall of Mirrors at Versailles, and that night the Wilsons took a train for the French coast. "It is finished," Woodrow told Edith wryly, "and, as no one is satisfied, it makes me hope we have made a just peace; but it is all in the lap of the gods."

Fighting for the Treaty

Wilson came home determined to convince the U.S. Senate and the people to approve the Treaty of Versailles. According to the Constitution, treaties must be ratified by a two-thirds majority in the Senate. On July 10, Wilson presented the treaty in the Senate chamber. "Dare we reject it and break the heart of the world?" he asked his audience.

When he had finished, the chamber rang with the applause of visitors and Democrats. Many of the Republicans, though, remained silent. They had strong reservations about letting the United States get too involved in international affairs. Nor were they the only ones who disliked the treaty. Liberals were disappointed that Wilson didn't achieve all Fourteen Points; German-Americans thought the treaty was unfair to Germany; isolationists of all political persuasions distrusted the idea of a League of Nations and didn't want the United States dragged into the problems of other nations.

The campaign against the treaty in the Senate was led by Massachusetts senator Henry Cabot Lodge, the Republican chairman of the Foreign Relations Committee and long-time Wilson foe. Lodge especially disliked Article 10, which called on members of the league to band together to protect any member that was threatened. He was determined to defeat both the treaty and the president, whom he despised as a woolly-headed idealist. Other more moderate Republicans would have been willing to vote for the treaty if only their reservations had been met, but Wilson refused to compromise. He was afraid that changes would weaken the league for which he had fought so hard. He would take his case to the people directly.

Against the advice of Edith and Dr. Grayson, who were worried about his health, Wilson decided to make a cross-country speaking tour. On the evening of September 2, 1919, Woodrow and Edith boarded their train, the Presidential Special, for an 8,000-mile (12,875 km) trip across the country. Traveling 400 miles (644 km) a day, Wilson made thirty-two speeches in twenty-two days. To large cheering crowds, he voiced his opinion that without the league "I can predict with absolute certainty that within another generation there will be another world war." Wilson was winning supporters, but he was not sleeping well and had a bad cough and frequent headaches.

Wilson debarks from a train in St. Paul, Minnesota, toward the beginning of his post-war speaking tour. At every stop, he made a speech from the rear platform of the train or the podium of a crowded, smoke-filled community hall. The frenetic schedule soon exhausted him, and he fell ill.

The Fallen Warrior

The night of September 25, 1919, Woodrow called Edith into his room and told her that he was ill and in pain. The next morning, after a sleepless night, it fell to Edith to tell her devastated husband that the trip was over; he was too sick to continue. They sped back to Washington. On October 2, a few days after they returned, Edith found Woodrow unconscious on the floor of the bathroom. He had suffered a massive stroke that paralyzed the left side of his body. For weeks afterward, he lay on the brink of death.

No one told the press or the people of the United States how seriously ill the president truly was. Edith believed that if Woodrow were forced to step down before the league was approved, the disappointment would kill him. Grayson announced that his patient was exhausted and overworked and required absolute rest but never mentioned the word stroke. On the advice of Dr. Dercum, one of the specialists who had been called in as an advisor, Edith resolved to keep as many problems as possible from Woodrow and deal with them herself. The only people she allowed into the sickroom were members of the family, doctors, and his secretary. Even Wilson's cabinet did not know the extent of his illness. In truth, for the first month of Wilson's illness, the executive branch of government virtually ceased to function.

Dr. Cary Grayson updates reporters on Woodrow Wilson's condition. Dr. Grayson attended Wilson as his personal physician throughout WIlson's entire presidency.

As Woodrow's health slowly improved, Edith acted as her husband's guardian. She read all government documents that came to his desk and decided which ones were important enough to ask him about. She gave him concise, informative reports, trying not to include any information that would upset him. "I never made a single decision regarding the disposition of public affairs," she once wrote. "The only decision that was mine was what was important, and what was not, and the very important decision of when to present matters to my husband." When he wanted to write a letter, Edith took dictation and guided his shaky hand to write his signature.

Inevitably, rumors flew about who was really in charge at the White House. Edith was called "The Presidentress," or "America's First Woman President." In December, a Senate **delegation** headed by Senator Albert Fall requested a meeting with Wilson to talk about a crisis in Mexico. They entered the president's bedroom to find him sitting up in bed wearing a sweater, his paralyzed left arm hidden under the bedclothes. "We have all been praying for you, Mr. President," Fall began.

"Which way, Senator?" Wilson said with a smile.

Clearly, Fall realized, the president was still in command of his faculties. As Fall discussed the Mexican situation, it also became apparent that he was up to date on foreign affairs. No one then or later suggested that it was time for Wilson to step down.

The Last Years in Office

In November 1919, meanwhile, the Treaty of Versailles and U.S. membership in the League of Nations came up for a vote and was defeated by the Senate. All would not have been lost, however, if either Lodge or Wilson had been willing to negotiate on Article 10. Most senators were willing to vote for the treaty, with amendments, and many historians argue that if Wilson had been his normal self he would have forged a political compromise. His stroke had impaired his judgment, however, and limited his mental flexibility. He dug in his heels and would not budge. "This is not a time for tactics," he told an aide. "It is a time to stand square. I can stand defeat. I cannot stand retreat from conscientious duty."

On March 19, 1920, the peace treaty came up for a vote again and went down to final defeat. "If I were not a Christian, I think I should go mad," Wilson told Grayson. "But my faith in God holds me to the belief that he is in some way working out his own plans." Not until 1921 would the United States finally sign a separate peace treaty with Germany. It never did join the League of Nations, which had limited influence without the power of the United States behind it.

During the last year of his presidency, Wilson spent most of his time in a wheelchair. He could walk only with help, his left leg dragging. Edith remained by his side, reading him memos, taking notes, and caring for him. Although his mind was sound, his attention span was brief, and he lacked strength for any new initiative. For the most part, the machinery of government ground on without him.

Wilson never seemed to realize just how ill he was and even clung to the hope of being elected for a third term. Edith was greatly relieved, though, when the Democrats chose Governor James Cox of Ohio to run for president in the 1920 election. Cox and his running mate, Franklin Delano Roosevelt, pledged to keep Wilson's dream of the League of Nations alive. When they were soundly beaten by Republicans Warren G. Harding and Calvin Coolidge in

Democratic presidential nominee Governor James M. Cox (second from right) and his running mate Franklin D. Roosevelt (third from right) on the campaign trail in 1920. They would lose the election to Warren G. Harding and Calvin Coolidge.

November, the Wilsons were disappointed. Still, the year ended on a high note for both of them when Woodrow was awarded the Nobel Peace Prize for 1919 for his role in founding the league.

The day of Harding's inauguration, Wilson was helped into his cutaway coat, gray trousers, and high hat and rode in an open carriage to the inauguration, "a slumped and frail figure." A few days before, as he said goodbye to his cabinet, he had started to cry. "Gentlemen," he said, pulling himself together, "it is one of the handicaps of my physical condition that I cannot control myself as I have been accustomed to do. God bless you all."

Peace with Honor

Woodrow and Edith moved into a house on S Street in Washington, D.C., where they lived very quietly for the next few years. They saw family members, rode in their Pierce-Arrow touring car with the

Wilson, seated beside Edith, acknowledges the applause of the crowd on Armistice Day (now called Veterans Day), 1921. The Wilsons were riding in a procession to honor an anonymous WWI soldier, who was buried that day in the Tomb of the Unknown Soldier in Arlington National Cemetery.

Princeton tiger on the hood, and sometimes went to the theater. Wilson wanted to write a book he had been planning for a long time called *The Philosophy of Politics*. He wrote a dedication to his wife, but he got no further. The sick man no longer had the ability to see his plan through, and the book was never written.

He participated yearly in Armistice Day events. On November 11, 1923, he addressed those who gathered on his doorstep to pay tribute to him, the man who had led them through the war. "Just one word more," he said before turning into the house. "I cannot refrain from saying it: I am not one of those that have the least anxiety about the triumph of the principles I have stood for. I have seen fools resist Providence before, and I have seen their destruction, as will come upon these again, utter destruction and contempt. That we shall prevail is as sure as that God reigns." To the last, Wilson remained defiant.

By early 1924, it was obvious that he was fading fast. "The machinery is broken," Wilson told Grayson. "I am ready." On February 3, 1924, as crowds of people kept silent vigil outside his bedroom, Woodrow Wilson died. His last word was "Edith."

Dr. Grayson, who had cared for his ailing body so long, summed up the meaning of Wilson's death: "He was as much a casualty of the war as any soldier who fell in the field. His death was a result of his consecration to the service of his country and humanity."

Wilson's casket is brought into Washington's National Cathedral on February 6, 1924. After the funeral service, Edith placed a spray of black orchids on Woodrow's coffin.

EDITH ALONE

Edith Wilson had been married to Woodrow for little more than eight years, but preserving his legacy occupied the remaining thirty-seven years of her life. At first desolated by his death, she spent her days sorting through mementos and clothes, trying to come to terms with her grief. Gradually she began to find new interests in life, to see friends and family and to travel. In 1925, she visited the new League of Nations headquarters in Geneva, Switzerland, and received a standing ovation. The applause was not for her, she knew, but for her husband and the ideas he stood for.

Ray Stannard Baker was Wilson's first biographer. He worked closely with Edith for years to organize and edit Wilson's papers.

Her primary responsibility was to prepare Wilson's papers for publication. In this daunting task she enlisted the aid of scholar and journalist Ray Stannard Baker, who would publish eleven volumes in all on Wilson's life and letters between 1927 and 1939. In March 1925, 67 cartons of papers were trucked from the house on S Street to Baker's office in Amherst, Massachusetts. Edith was supportive of all Baker's work, and he complimented her as "one of the most competent and conscientious people [he] had ever known." She did disagree with his assessment of Woodrow immediately after his first wife's death, however. Baker seemed to her to dwell excessively on Woodrow's overwhelming grief. It was understandably difficult for Edith, who had known such a fulfilling relationship with Woodrow, to comprehend that her husband had been deeply in love twice in his life.

An Honored Life

When Democrat Franklin D. Roosevelt was elected president in 1932, Edith rode in his inaugural parade. On December 8, 1941,

Edith Wilson (center) chats with First Lady Eleanor Roosevelt (left) and Wilson's former secretary of war Josephus Daniels (ambassador to Mexico under Franklin D. Roosevelt) at a Washington, D.C., dinner on January 20, 1945.

she sat next to Eleanor Roosevelt in the visitor's gallery of Congress as Roosevelt asked for a declaration of war. World War II saw her once again at work for the Red Cross, sewing for the soldiers. She was delighted when the United Nations was founded in 1945, considering it a continuation of her husband's work.

Edith continued to enjoy life as she got older and was thrilled in 1961 when John F. Kennedy, too, invited her to join his inaugural procession. Though the temperature that day was below freezing, she rode in an open car, a happy smile on her face. A year later, in October 1961, she attended a ceremony at the White House to witness Kennedy establishing a commission to plan a Woodrow Wilson memorial. Afterward, the president turned and offered her the pen he had used to sign the document. "I didn't dare ask you for it," she said, and everyone laughed. No one had ever thought of Edith Wilson as meek.

On December 28, 1961, Edith was due to attend a dedication of the new Woodrow Wilson Bridge over the Potomac River in Washington. She was determined to be there, despite the freezing weather and her own failing health. But early that morning her heart failed, and she slipped away. Edith Bolling Galt Wilson was eighty-nine years old.

TIME LINE

1856	Thomas Woodrow Wilson born on December 28
1858	Wilson family moves to Augusta, Georgia
1860	Ellen Louise Axson born on May 15
1861	Civil War starts
1865	Civil War ends
1870	Wilson family moves to Columbia, South Carolina
1872	Edith Bolling born on October 15
1873	Woodrow goes to Davidson College
1875	Woodrow attends College of New Jersey at Princeton
1879	Woodrow goes to University of Virginia Law School
1883	Woodrow attends graduate school at Johns Hopkins
1885	Woodrow marries Ellen Axson on June 24; Woodrow begins teaching at Bryn Mawr College
1886	Margaret Axson Wilson born on April 16
1887	Jessie Woodrow Wilson born on August 28
1888	Woodrow begins teaching at Wesleyan University
1889	Eleanor Randolph Wilson born October 5
1890	Woodrow begins teaching at Princeton University
1896	Edith Bolling marries Norman Galt on April 30
1902	Woodrow becomes president of Princeton
1908	Edith becomes a widow
1910	Woodrow elected governor of New Jersey
1912	Woodrow elected president of the United States on November 5
1914	Archduke Franz Ferdinand and wife assassinated on June 28; Germany declares war on Russia on August 1 and on France on August 3; Ellen Axson Wilson dies on August 6
1915	*Lusitania* sunk on May 7; Woodrow and Edith meet in March; Woodrow marries Edith Bolling Galt on December 18
1916	Pershing crosses into Mexico on March 15; Wilson reelected as president on November 7; National Defense Act passed
1917	Russian Revolution begins; United States declares war on Germany on April 6
1918	Woodrow delivers Fourteen Points speech on January 8; Armistice ends war on November 11; Woodrow and Edith leave for Paris Peace Conference on December 4
1919	Treaty of Versailles signed on June 28; Woodrow suffers stroke on October 2; Senate rejects treaty on November 19; Woodrow wins Nobel Peace Prize
1920	Senate rejects treaty again on March 19; Nineteenth Amendment gives women the vote on August 18; Warren Harding elected president; Woodrow and Edith move to house on S Street
1924	Woodrow Wilson dies on February 3
1961	Edith Bolling Galt Wilson dies on December 28

GLOSSARY

colonial—relating to a territory and group of people that are governed by a separate, remote country.

communist—person who believes in a system of government in which one political party holds power and property is owned by the government or community as a whole.

conservative—viewpoint that supports traditional values or institutions and does not favor taking chances or risks.

czar—person with great power and control; a title given to Russian rulers before 1917.

delegation—group of people officially chosen to speak or act for others.

democracy—form of government in which power rests with the people, either directly or through elected representatives.

disarmament—reduction in a country's military force or weapons.

dyslexic—(dyslexia) learning disability characterized by difficulty reading or recognizing letters.

electoral college—group of people chosen from each state that gives the official vote for the president of the United States, based on the results of the popular vote held in each state.

encephalitis—inflammation of the brain, caused by any of several infectious diseases.

entrenchments—area that is defended and surrounded by trenches, or ditches.

financier—person who is skilled in raising or spending public money, usually on a large scale.

inauguration—ceremony at which a public official, especially a president, is sworn into office.

incumbent—official who currently holds a political office.

interest rates—charges that a financial institution sets for borrowing money, usually a percentage of the amount loaned.

isolationist—belief in a policy of noninvolvement with other nations.

magna carta—any document granting basic rights or liberties. The original Magna Carta was the document King John of England signed in 1215, which granted personal and political liberties to the English people.

militaristic autocracy—nation ruled by one person who controls by using military force.

monopoly—complete control over a service or product within a given area; companies that exert such control.

parish—defined region that is given its own Christian church and priest or minister.

primary—preliminary election in the United States in which members of each political party vote for a candidate to run for president in the general election.

progressive—in favor of social progress or change.

ratify—act of approving formally.

seminary—school for training men and women for work as ministers, priests, or rabbis.

shorthand—system of writing used to record speech quickly. Simple symbols are used to represent sounds, words, or phrases.

slum—crowded, rundown area of a city where poor people live.

Speaker of the House—person who heads the political party (Democrat or Republican) which has the most members in the U.S. House of Representatives and so controls it.

tuberculosis—contagious disease that attacks mainly the lungs.

U-boat—German submarine.

FURTHER INFORMATION

Further Reading

Adams, Simon. *Eyewitness: World War I*. (Eyewitness Books). New York: Dorling Kindersley, 2004.

Brill, Marlene Targ. *Let Women Vote*. (Spotlight on American History). Brookfield, CT: Milbrook Press, 1995.

Bosco, Peter I., Antoinette Bosco, and John S. Bowman. *World War I*. (America at War). New York: Facts on File, 2003.

Dubovoj, Sina. *Ellen A. Wilson: The Woman Who Made a President*. (Presidential Wives). Hauppauge, NY: Nova Science Publishers, 2004.

Flanagan, Alice K. *Edith Bolling Galt Wilson*: 1872–1971. (Encyclopedia of First Ladies). New York: Children's Press, 1999.

Gaines, Ann. *Woodrow Wilson*. (Great American Presidents). New York: Chelsea House, 2003.

Gormley, Beatrice. *First Ladies: Women Who Called the White House Home*. Madison, WI: Turtleback Books, 2004.

Gould, Lewis L. *American First Ladies: Their Lives and Their Legacy*. New York: Routledge, 2001.

Green, Robert. *Woodrow Wilson*. (Profiles of the Presidents). Minneapolis: Compass Point Books, 2003.

Hakim, Joy. *War, Peace, and All That Jazz*. (A History of Us, Vol. 9). New York: Oxford University Press, 1995.

Holden, Henry M. *Woodrow Wilson*. (Presidents). Springfield, NJ: Enslow, 2003.

Mayo, Edith P. (ed). *The Smithsonian Book of First Ladies: Their Lives, Times and Issues*. New York: Henry Holt/ Smithsonian Institution, 1996.

McLynn, Frank. *Villa and Zapata: A History of the Mexican Revolution*. New York: Carrol & Graf Publishers, 2002.

Ross, Stewart. *Leaders of World War I*. (World Wars). London: Hodder Children's Books, 2002.

Schlesinger, Arthur Meier, Jr. (ed.) *The Election of 1912 and the Administration of Woodrow Wilson*. (Major Presidential Elections and the Administrations That Followed). Broomall, PA: Mason Crest, 2003.

Schraff, Anne. *Woodrow Wilson*. (United States Presidents). Springfield, NJ: Enslow, 1998.

Uschan, Michael V. *A Multicultural Portrait of World War I*. (Perspectives). New York: Benchmark Books, 1995.

Uschan, Michael V. *The 1910s*. (A Cultural History of the United States Through the Decades). San Diego: Lucent, 1999.

FURTHER INFORMATION

Places to Visit

The Boyhood Home of President
Woodrow Wilson
419 Seventh Street
Augusta, GA 30901
(706) 722-9828

The National First Ladies' Library
Education and Research Center
205 Market Avenue South
Canton, OH 44702
(330) 452-0876

Smithsonian National Museum of
American History
14th Street and Constitution Ave. N.W.
Washington, D.C. 20013
(202) 633-1000

White House
1600 Pennsylvania Avenue, N.W.
Washington, D.C. 20500
(202) 456-7041

Wilson Gravesite
Washington National Cathedral
Massachusetts and Wisconsin Ave., N.W.
Washington, D.C. 20016
(202) 537-6200

Woodrow Wilson Birthplace and Museum
18-24 North Coalter Street
Staunton, VA 24402
(540) 885-0897

Woodrow Wilson House
2340 S Street, N.W.
Washington, D.C. 20008
(202) 387-4062

Web Sites

Internet Public Library, Presidents of
   the United States (IPL POTUS)
www.ipl.org/div/potus/wwilson.html

The National First Ladies' Library
www.firstladies.org

PBS American Experience:
Woodrow Wilson
www.pbs.org/wgbh/amex/wilson

The White House
www.whitehouse.gov

Woodrow Wilson House
www.woodrowwilsonhouse.org

Woodrow Wilson International
   Center for Scholars
www.wwics.si.edu

INDEX

Page numbers in **bold** represent photographs.

About the Author

Ruth Ashby has written many award-winning biographies and
nonfiction books for children, including *Herstory, The Elizabethan
Age,* and *Pteranodon: The Life Story of a Pterosaur.* She lives on Long
Island with her husband, daughter, and dog, Nubby.

www.ingramcontent.com/pod-product-compliance
Lightning Source LLC
Chambersburg PA
CBHW040855100426

42813CB00015B/2805